AF531195

ANIMALS IN HOT AND COLD HABITATS

Contents

Written by Cristiano Bertolucci and Francesco Milo
Illustrations by Alessandro Bartolozzi

WATERBIRD BOOKS
Columbus, Ohio

The Sonoran Desert in Arizona is very hot, and it rarely rains. Cactuses, which have adapted to the shortage of water, grow in the sandy soil. Their long roots stretch down to find water deep underground. The cactuses' tough skins help hold in the little water that they absorb.

Cactuses are vital to the animals living in the Sonoran Desert. Their flowers and nectar feed the animals of the desert. The elf owl digs its nests in cactuses. The spines on the cactus help protect the animal from predators, and the nest stays cool.

Some animals, like the desert mouse and burrowing owl, nest underground for protection. Others, like the slow tortoise, hide in the thick shells on their backs. The skunk protects itself by spraying predators with a foul-smelling liquid.

Use the gatefold pages in the center of the book to find the answers to the following questions:

- Which animals in this picture can fly?
- How do desert animals protect themselves from the heat?
- What is the name of the snake in this picture?

Not all deserts are scorching hot. It rarely rains on the wide Asian Desert, but it is very cold. Only a little grass and some low bushes grow there.

The Asian Desert is home to several large herbivores, or animals that eat only plants, like the goitered gazelle on the left. The Przewalskii wild horse looks over the land, while an onager grazes. A saiga antelope stands near the camel. The camel, like the other mammals in this desert, has a thick coat to protect it from the cold.

Many smaller mammals live underground. A marmot and

a white-spotted ground squirrel peek from their burrows, while a blind mole rat and a hamster stay hidden.

A kangaroo mouse hops on the rocks near a bird, called a *stone curlew*. An eagle flies overhead, while the bird with the spotted chest, called a *buteo-buteo*, perches on a rock.

Use the gatefold pages in the center of the book to find the answers to the following questions:

- What is the name of the animal that looks like a cat?
- What other animals can you identify?
- Which animals are not mammals?

The hot, grass-covered plains of South America are known as the *pampas*. Small animals, like mice and other rodents, burrow underground here to escape the heat. Others, like the ovenbird, design their nests with roofs that give them shade.

The lean, black-footed maned wolf is smaller than most other types of wolves. It is fast, but not as fast as the silver-plumed greater rhea. The rhea looks like a small ostrich, but is not related to it. Like an ostrich, it cannot fly. Many other birds on the pampas can fly, though, like

the burrowing owl peeking out of its nest and the uccello gallito with the red crest.

An armadillo and a long-nosed anteater hunt for insects. They have sharp claws that they use to dig into the ground and tear apart the insect nests they find.

Use the gatefold pages in the center of the book to find the answers to the following questions:

- Which animals are mammals?
- Which animals are birds?
- Do these animals live in other habitats?

The tundra is a plain that lies just below the Arctic Circle. Snow covers the ground most of the year. Insects swarm during the tundra's short, cool summer. The insects help pollinate the tundra grasses and the other plants that the reindeer and European elk eat.

During the winter, when it snows, many animals grow thick, white fur to camouflage themselves, so they blend in with the background. Some camouflaged animals, like the snowshoe hare, are *prey* because they are hunted. Others, like the snow owl behind the hare, are hunters, or *predators*.

Some animals are both predator and prey. The ermine is related to the weasel. It hunts mice and rodents that live under the snow. The ermine is not the only predator in the tundra. The large wolf, an Arctic fox, the snow owl, and even large and hungry ravens, are predators on the tundra.

Use the gatefold pages in the center of the book to find the answers to the following questions:

- Which animals are reptiles?
- How is the European elk different from the reindeer?
- What is the name of the white bird with the black head?

India is hot and tropical. This slow-moving Indian river is home to many animals. On the bank, a clouded leopard crouches on a branch. A tapir, recognizable by its long nose, steps into the river. Indian buffaloes wallow in the muddy water near a water hen. A poisonous king cobra and a mongoose fight. Both are incredibly fast. The winner will eat the loser.

Some animals swimming in the river are dangerous, like the gharials, which resemble crocodiles. Others, like the kissing gourami, are harmless. A softshell turtle

swims near a long-nosed river dolphin. The dolphin belongs to the Cetacean family, or group of mammals that live in water. It has adapted to living in the muddy river. Since it probably cannot see much in the muddy water, it has developed a keen sense of hearing.

Use the gatefold pages in the center of the book to find the answers to the following questions:

- What is the bird with red plumage called?
- Which animals are insects?
- Which animals are reptiles?

Canada's clear, cold rivers are filled with animals. A loon floats on a beaver pool. Beavers build dams across fast-moving water, blocking the water to make large pools and waterfalls. Beavers are powerful swimmers, using their flat tails as paddles. If a beaver sees something dangerous, it smacks the water hard with its tail. At that sound, all the beavers in the area dive deep into the water.

Many different types of fish live in the river. Every year, salmon swim upstream against the current and jump over waterfalls to the place where they were born. When they

reach it, the female salmon lays eggs that will be fertilized by a male salmon. Otters and grizzly bears commonly eat salmon. This makes the salmon's trip even more hazardous.

Use the gatefold pages in the center of the book to find the answers to the following questions:

- Which animals can fly?
- How do these animals stay warm?
- What are the names of the other fish you see here?

Pallas's cat
Saiga
Hamster
Marten
Leopard seal
Crabeater seal
Sea elephant
Tree-kangaroo
Marmot
Lemming
Wolverine
Southern fur seal
Ground squirrel
Flying squirrel
Gray squirrel
Weasel
Bat
Bactrian camel
Clouded leopard
Lynx
Beaver
European squirrel
European elk
Mouse
Reindeer
Peccary
Otter
Chinchilla
Indian buffalo
Racoon
Fox
Arctic hare
Pronghorn
Weddel seal
Desert mouse
Cuscus
Field mouse
Echidna
Mara
Przewalski's horse
Brown bear
Mongoose
Wolf
Arctic fox

its larger cousins on the Australian plains, the tree-kangaroo is a marsupial. Marsupials are mammals that carry their young, which are born very early, in pouches. The spotted cuscus is also a marsupial.

Use the gatefold pages in the center of the book to find the answers to the following questions:

- What is the small animal covered in quills?
- Which animals are insects?
- What is the bird with the curled tail?

Vast forests grow in cold Siberia. The trees are tall and have thick bark. Plant colors are muted and less flashy than in the tropical forests.

Many birds live here, like the Lapland owl and the green and yellow goldcrests, which are perched on branches. The red crossbill's beak is specially designed to open pine cones to reach and eat the seeds. A sparrow-hawk dives through the air at a European squirrel eating a seed.

Mammals, like the squirrel, have thick coats of fur to protect them from the cold. Some, like the yellow-eyed

lynx and the fox, are hunted for their coats. The weasel and sharp-clawed marten are swift, clever hunters. The wolverine, with its sharp teeth and claws, is a fierce fighter. It is not large, but it is one of the most dangerous animals in the world.

Use the gatefold pages in the center of the book to find the answers to the following questions:

- Which animals are mammals?
- What mammal is gliding between the trees?
- What is the small, yellow bird landing on a branch?

Animals flourish in the warm blue waters and on the hot shores of the Mediterranean Sea. Gulls swoop in the air. A green turtle lays its eggs in the sand.

Tube worms, sea stars, and mollusks live under the sand or reef. Tiny animals called *corals* build the reef. When they die, their skeletons become part of the reef. A red lobster climbs on the corals. A hermit crab also scurries along the reef. Hermit crabs do not grow their own shells. They protect their soft bodies by moving into shells that other animals have abandoned. This crab put two stinging

anemones on its shell for protection, which can paralyze small sea animals.

Farther out from shore, an octopus wriggles out of its cave. A sea turtle dives after fish. A jellyfish trails tentacles like a net to stun and trap passing fish.

Use the gatefold pages in the center of the book to find the answers to the following questions:

- How do Caspian and Mediterranean gulls differ?
- Which animals are fish?
- Which animals are mammals?

The icy coastal waters of the Antarctic are rich in nutrients and tiny organisms. They provide food for tiny fish and krill. Krill are tiny crustaceans, like shrimp. The huge southern right whale eats only plankton, krill, and other tiny animals. It cannot eat anything larger because it has baleen plates instead of teeth, which act like a filter across the whale's mouth, allowing only small sea animals to pass through the plates.

Killer whales grow to about 30 feet long, about the same length as a school bus, and they commonly eat

seals, smaller whales, and dolphins.

Birds, like penguins, cormorants, and the black-footed albatrosses, also eat the fish and krill. Penguins swim well, but cannot fly. Many other sea animals are at home in the cold Antarctic waters.

Use the gatefold pages in the center of the book to find the answers to the following questions:

- Which animals are mammals?
- How are the seals like the sea elephants?
- How are the seals different from each other?

DoGi
A DoGi spa publication

Original title Caldo e freddo
Text Cristiano Bertolucci and Francesco Milo
Illustrations Alessandro Bartolozzi
Original concept Sebastiano Ranchetti
Graphic design Sebastiano Ranchetti
Layout Sansai Zappini
Translation Jeremy Carden
Art direction Andrea Rauch

This edition published in the United States of America in 2003 by
Waterbird Books
an imprint of McGraw-Hill Children's Publishing,
a Division of The McGraw-Hill Companies
8787 Orion Place
Columbus, Ohio 43240-4027

www.MHkids.com

Library of Congress Cataloging-in-Publication Data on file with the publisher.

Edited in the U.S. by Joanna Callihan, Nathan Hemmelgarn, and Carol Ottolenghi.

Printed and bound in Eurolitho SpA
Cesano Boscone - Milan - Italy

1-57768-526-1

1 2 3 4 5 6 7 8 9 10 DGS 09 08 07 06 05 04 03

The McGraw-Hill Companies